A Treatise on Bringing Children to Jesus Christ

A Treatise on Bringing Children to Jesus Christ

A MEDIEVAL CLASSIC

Translated from the Latin of
John Charlier Gerson

by W. Whitty
(Translator of "Let us go to the Holy Table")

With a new Introduction by James D. Smith, III

WIPF & STOCK · Eugene, Oregon

A TREATISE ON BRINGING CHILDREN TO
CHRIST
By Gerson, John Charlier and Whitty, W.

Wipf and Stock Publishers
199 W 8th Ave, Suite 3
Eugene, OR 97401

ISBN 13: 978-1-5326-6359-8
Publication date 10/05/2018
Previously published by M. H. Gill & Son, 1899

Cover Image: "Christ Blessing the Children," painted (oil on panel) by Lucas Cranach the Elder (1472-1553) in 1537. Though from the Reformation era, a generation after Gerson's first printed editions, it's chosen here as one of Europe's earliest paintings of Jesus ministering to children.

Contents

Introduction to the 2018 Reprint Edition by Rev. James D. Smith III, Th.D. | vii

A Treatise on Bringing the Little Children to Jesus Christ | 1

FIRST REFLECTION. | 5

How necessary it is for Children to come to Christ; how advantageous for themselves and for the Church.

SECOND REFLECTION. | 13

Of those who scandalise Little Children, and prevent them in so many ways from coming to Christ.

THIRD REFLECTION. | 23

Of the commendable zeal of those who conduct Children along the path which leads to Christ.

FOURTH REFLECTION. | 37

An apologetic for our own ministry in regard of Children, together with an appeal to them to come to Christ through the medium of that ministry humble though it be.

Introduction to the 2018 Reprint Edition

IN 1962, PHILIPPE ARIES' *L'enfant et la vie familiale sous l'ancien regime* (1960) appeared in English as *Centuries of Childhood: A Social History of Family Life*. Though George Henry Payne's *The Child in Human Progress* (1916) offered the first such published history, Aries work became the foundation and catalyst for all future discussions. A central thesis was that childhood was not a recognized and valued phase of human existence until the 17th century, and that "in medieval society the idea of childhood did not exist." As engaged by scholars such as Adrian Wilson, Anastasia Ulanowicz, and especially Nicholas Orme (*Medieval Children*, 2001), both epiphanies and controversies have followed.

Reflecting this, in May of 1982 a "Conference on Religion and the Family in Medieval and Early Modern Europe" drew an ardent crowd of scholars to Harvard Divinity School. Inspired by HDS historian Clarissa Atkinson, I served as co-organizer with doctoral colleague Klaus Lindner—and six papers appeared in the *Journal of Family History* (Summer, 1983). Among the speakers was

A Treatise on Bringing Children to Christ

David Herlihy, whose "The Making of the Medieval Family: Symmetry, Structure and Sentiment" brought an enthusiastic response. His treatment, and conversations with him as a student, first drew my attention to medieval theologian Jean Gerson (1363-1429).

Most recently, Brian Patrick McGuire's masterful *Jean Gerson and the Last Medieval Reformation* (2005) has portrayed him as Chancellor of the University of Paris, an advocate of reconciliation and Catholic reform with views not fully embraced by the Council of Constance, and one whose personal crises inspired an affective theology deserving the honor *Doctor Christianissimus*. Aries saw Gerson largely as Schoolmaster, whose "regulations are interesting for the moral ideal which they reveal"—influencing the "moralists and strict pedagogues" of the 17th century. Herlihy recognized Gerson as policy-maker, but more as prayerful devotee of three persons in the Holy Family: "Oh, venerable trinity—Jesus, Joseph and Mary—which divinity has joined, the concord of love!" Herlihy noted this *concordia charitatis* as his cultural and emotional ideal—and (in our conversations) that which underlies a classic Gerson work which Aries ignores: *De parvulis ad Christum trahendis*.

To this treatise, Gerson brings a wealth of insights from Greek and Latin sources, but keys his four arguments to Scripture. First, that in welcoming and loving children we follow Jesus (Matt. 19:14). Secondly, that judgment awaits any who wound the little ones, beloved in heaven (Matt 18:5-10). Thirdly—in a world plagued by sin—avenues of catechism, encouragement, teaching and confession rightly ministered bring healing (James 5: 16, 20). Finally, the mark of spiritual life is uplifting neighbors in difficulty where they are, practicing humility with one another (Galatians 6:1). To those who accused Gerson of wasting time on children, he brought spirited defense.

His closing word: "To the glory of that celestial Kingdom we are all invited—we who ought, every one of us, to be children in mind and heart—we are invited by Christ himself, who as well by the outward word of his truth as by the interior inspiration of his grace unceasingly cries out to us "Let the children come to Me."

The exact date of *De Trahendis* is uncertain. Surviving Latin texts date from the 1470s. The translator of this English edition, the Rev. William Whitty, dated it to Gerson's years in Lyons after 1419. There, at the Monastery of the Celestines, he catechized, educated and heard the confessions of school children. On the other hand, McGuire suggests 1406, which places it four years after Gerson's *De Vita Spirituali Anime*—one of the first attempts to articulate and defend modern natural rights theory. Either setting could readily occasion a work such as this.

A Treatise on Bringing Children to Christ

The present volume offers a faithful text of this classic to English readers for the first time since the 19th century. Its presentation is made possible by the John J. Burns Library, Boston College. Their intent is to make a digital presentation, including translator's original prefaces and appendices, available shortly. The shared hope is that these materials will both illustrate historic Christian expressions valuing children and the family, and resource more faithful reflection and action in our needy world today.

Rev. James D. Smith III, Th.D.
Bethel Seminary San Diego
La Jolla Christian Fellowship
Feast of the Guardian Angels, 2018

A Treatise on Bringing the Little Children to Jesus Christ

Suffer the Little Children, and forbid them not to come to me; for the kingdom of heaven is for such.

Our Supreme Law-giver and Teacher Jesus Christ has, by His instructions and the example of His life, bequeathed to His Church a body of doctrine, which will suffice for all time for the guidance of the faithful of every age and condition; of this our holy faith assures us,

And since children and youths constitute no insignificant portion of the Church, He has not been without making adequate provision for them as well as for others. For children, indeed, He would seem to be specially solicitous. To such lengths does He carry His zeal and tenderness in their regard that His divine anger is always certain to be aroused whenever any one is rash enough to prevent them from coming to Him, whether this be done from pride, harshness, severity, imprudence, thoughtlessness or any other cause. "Prevent not," He says, "the little children from coming to Me."

And as if to justify Himself for this indignant zeal of His on behalf of children, He gives at once this weighty and all-sufficient reason, a reason verily divine—"For the kingdom of heaven is for such."

St. Mark, when narrating the event which gave rise to this expression of the Saviour, says—"And the disciples rebuked those that brought them (the children); which when Jesus saw, He was much displeased, and saith to them, "Suffer the little children to come to me, and forbid them not;" and then, continues the Evangelist, "Jesus embracing them, and laying His hands upon them, blessed them."

These weighty and suggestive expressions of our Lord and the sacred writer, when duly considered, will be seen to convey a severe rebuke to those, no matter who they be, who in any way set themselves against the spiritual interests of children; who by any means whatever prevent them from coming to their Saviour. And, indeed, well do all such persons merit rebuke.

However, let us not, when we undertake to champion the cause of children, give way to any bitterness of feeling or severity of invective; let us rather imitate the gentle and simple ways of children themselves, in this following the example of the Saviour, who even, while angry with His disciples administered His reproof to them in the mildest and gentlest terms, merely saying to them, "Suffer the little children to come to me."

In fine, when pleading on their behalf, let us regulate our language in accordance with the nature and dispositions of children themselves, not being anxious to use the language of contention and disputation, or even the ordinary style of human speech, but being ready, if need be, to lisp and babble in our words as mothers and nurses are wont to do when they speak with little ones. If only we make ourselves understood in what we say we shall be quite content. The object we have in view is, not to argue, not to convict others of error, much less to cast ridicule upon them; but merely to bring forward certain reasons why children should come to Christ, and to remove, as far as may be, those obstacles which, unhappily, but too often prevent them from coining to Him.

We shall, therefore, in the following little work be as simple, clear and orderly as we can, dividing it for this purpose into four chapters, or, as we shall call them, reflections.

In the first we shall endeavour to show how necessary it is for children to come to Christ; how beneficial for themselves and for the Church.

In the second we shall speak of those who scandalise children; who in so many ways prevent them from coming to Christ.

In the third we shall treat of the commendable zeal of those, who labour to conduct children along the path that leads to Christ.

The fourth will be an apology for our own personal ministry in regard to children, together with an appeal to the little ones to continue to come to the Saviour through means of that ministry, humble though it be.

All that I shall say, particularly in this latter part of the book, I unreservedly submit to the kind and considerate judgment of my superiors. Nor do I desire in anything I shall say to lay stress on any opinion or wisdom of my own but choose rather to be guided by the prudent counsel of my spiritual friends, in this way tempering my zeal, such as it is, by a spirit of humility, that so it may not cause me to run into any indiscreet excess. As long, however, as these my good friends are with me in what I say, I shall easily disregard all that narrow-minded or evil-meaning men may put forward against me, knowing that one can come to Christ, to use the words of St. Jerome, "as well by bad as by good repute."

FIRST REFLECTION.

How necessary it is for Children to come to Christ; how advantageous for themselves and for the Church.

"It is good for a man to have borne the yoke from his youth." The yoke here referred to is identical with that of which Our Blessed Saviour speaks when He says that "His yoke is sweet and His burden light."

The reason it is so advantageous to have borne this yoke from the days of childhood is easily understood; for the sooner one takes it up, and the more earnest one is in carrying it, the more abundant is the grace given to the soul; and we know the more grace there is in the soul the more is the soul itself helped, strengthened, and nourished.

On the other hand, if a person does not put on this yoke at an early age, if he does not correspond with grace at a season when he is so capable of corresponding with it, if on the contrary he rejects and despises it, the inevitable consequence will be that by a just judgment from the Almighty he will forfeit all claim to the divine favours in later life. But then if God withdraws his graces from him, what is to become of him? The simple truth is, he cannot he saved; he cannot by possibility live the supernatural life; he must inevitably go headlong into sin.

You think perhaps that it is too difficult for you to attain to Christian virtue while you are yet young, yet pure and innocent; if so, how will it be with you when you are older, when your innocence shall have been frittered away and lost, when you shall have become estranged from your Creator, when you shall find yourself burthened, perhaps, and broken with a very load of vices and sins; how little will you then be able to practise or acquire the virtues of a Christian?

The first-fruits of the season, whether from the garden, the vineyard or the field, are the most acceptable offering to give to a friend. Even so it is with the service which souls give to God in the spring-time of life; such service is much more pleasing to Him than that which is given in later years, when, alas! people turn to Him, not so much because they are desirous for His sake to relinquish their sins, as because these sins have ceased to possess any longer attractions for them.

"With us, unhappy mortals," says the poet, "that portion of life which is the most excellent and precious is the first to pass away." This better and more excellent portion, therefore, it is that we ought to consecrate to the Almighty, and not the comparatively valueless dregs of a decrepid and languishing old age.

And in truth what other lesson than this does the Scripture intend to convey to us when it says that

FIRST REFLECTION.

the most acceptable and "most perfect praise" which God receives is that which comes to Him "from the lips and hearts *of the young.*"

Moreover, if we take into account the force of habit, which according to Aristotle is a sort of second nature, it will be seen that nothing can be more galling to the soul, and nothing more wicked and detestable in itself, than a habit of vice; while, on the other hand, there is nothing more sweet or agreeable, nothing more divine, than a habit of virtue. And hence it is that we have the philosophers and poets unanimously agreeing with the theologians, that *nothing can be of greater importance* than that souls should exert themselves *while yet young* to root all evil out of their hearts, and implant in its stead good and virtuous dispositions.

"Habit," says Virgil, "is everything for the youthful mind."

And Cicero lays down the principle that everyone should labour to be virtuous from the very beginning, remarking at the same time that though virtue be at first irksome and difficult, yet practice will soon make it easy and pleasant

"What you can in the beginning but ill bear," says Ovid, "accustom yourself to it, and you will soon be able to put up with it easily enough."

And with him Horace entirely agrees; for he Says—"Train the steed while he is yet young and he will afterwards be obedient to the rider's hand; let the young hound see from time to time the skin or even the image of the prey, and he will begin ere long to hunt the prey itself in the woods. So also must it be with you, young person, whoever you be; whatever habits you would wish to be yours in later life, these you must begin to cultivate from the very commencement; if you want to be virtuous then you must learn to be virtuous now; nor need you be afraid that the virtue you acquire in the days of your youth will afterwards easily abandon you, for virtue once acquired always clings, like as the odour of a perfume continues to adhere to the vase which once contained it."

Finally, if, as Averroes relates, the force of habit is clearly and terribly witnessed in the iniquitous customs and the sacrilegious superstitions which hold sway in certain nations, if It appears also in the case of persons, who, like Saint Augustine and so many others, have become the slaves of vice, may not its power be demonstrated even more strikingly still in those who, enjoying all the advantages of the true religion, accustom themselves to the virtues which it teaches, and who, as remarked before, have the good dispositions they are daily acquiring continually augmented and strengthened by the all-powerful graces so plentifully bestowed upon them from on high?

There is a certain false and pernicious proverb which, I confess, I can never hear but with sentiments of disgust and abhorrence—"Angel in youth, reprobate in age." If there were the slightest truth in

FIRST REFLECTION.

this saying; if he who from the first struggles against the evil tendencies of human nature and tries to break down their power is afterwards likely to fall away and become the slave of Satan, what then is to be expected of him who begins at an early age to indulge his evil propensities, and who as time goes on superadds to these propensities all the fearful tyranny of vicious habits? Must not such a one be infinitely more likely to become "a reprobate in age" than the other?

Impious as this adage is, yet it has found a certain amount of credence among the unthinking multitude; and to what purpose? To serve, unfortunately, as an encouragement to wicked youths to continue in their evil ways, and to prevent them being checked and corrected by the edifying example of their more virtuous companions, who, alas! lie under this double disadvantage—that they are everywhere the fewer in number, and are very frequently too weak and too inconstant to maintain their good and edifying conduct, in presence of and in opposition to the wicked and scandalous example of their associates.

And after all what wonder is it that the corrupt and wicked children should be so numerous, and the innocent and virtuous so few? How could it be otherwise? For do we not see on every side things sanctioned and commended in children which should be utterly reprobated and condemned in them—pride and vanity; haughtiness of look and bearing; profanity, frivolity and obscenity in conversation; worldliness, effeminacy, sensuality in all their forms; when such things as these are permitted, when they are even encouraged in children, what is to be expected of them or how can they turn out in after life? Alas! the present deplorable condition of Christian society gives to the question but too melancholy an answer.

He certainly was a wise and enlightened man, and not in the least in error, who maintained that the best and most effectual way to improve the morals of the faithful generally was to make a beginning with the children. Children being more innocent than others, or at all events not having vice so deeply rooted in them, are much more susceptible of Christian discipline and training; not, indeed, that they are not as children subject to a certain drawback or defectiveness in this respect, for it must be confessed they are; and it is to this that Aristotle refers when he says that children are inapt learners of moral science (though by this latter observation he by no means intends to insinuate that it is useless to teach it to them, for in such case he would be contradicting himself, having already asserted in his writings that it *is* useful, and even necessary, to do so.)

Children, however, notwithstanding the natural infirmity of their young minds, are gifted with a special aptitude for taking in the primary ideas and principles of good, above all when they have not

FIRST REFLECTION.

been permitted to become already imbued with any false or unsound ideas, when as yet no vicious maxims have been allowed to take root in their hearts. As new bottles are the best and most suitable for holding good and costly wines, so the minds of children are the best and fittest receptacles for primary Christian truths; and as trees that are young are the most pliable to the gardener's hand, so children are of all others the most easily moulded and trained to good and virtuous habits.

Very different is it with those who are older and whose habits have been already formed; with difficulty can they be changed or moulded; you may "break such, but you will scarcely bend them." "If the Ethiopian," says the prophet Jeremias, "can change his skin, or the leopard his spots, you also may do well when you have learned evil."

Now, if, as we have been showing, the reformation add improvement of morals ought to begin with the children, where, I ask, could such a sacred and salutary work he better initiated than in the city of Paris? The children of that celebrated centre will come in the course of time to be largely dispersed throughout Christendom, and hence if they are only properly brought up and trained they cannot help but be the source of very widespread good in the world, being the means of enlightening and edifying many both in their own and other countries, but especially in their own.

From all we have laid down in the foregoing reflection one conclusion strictly follows; it is this—that no one should ever dare, either by word or deed, either openly or secretly, to throw an obstacle in the way of the fulfilment of the mandate of the Saviour—"Suffer the little children to come to me;" and he who presumes to do so is the enemy of the church, labours for her overthrow, and prepares in some measure the way for the reign of Antichrist on earth.

SECOND REFLECTION.

Of those who scandalise Little Children, and prevent them in so many ways from coming to Christ.

"He that shall scandalise one of these little ones that believe in Me, it were better for him that a millstone would be hanged about his neck, and that he should be drowned in the depth of the sea."

We are not to understand the "little ones" here mentioned as referring only to those who are children in the spiritual sense, but must take the words in their literal meaning as referring to children properly so called. Indeed we must understand them primarily and principally of *children*, who from their simplicity and inexperience are more open to scandal and more likely to be ruined by it than others.

"The child," says Horace, "is like soft wax, which easily takes an impression; only, unfortunately, he is more likely to be impressed by evil than by good; and," he adds, "let the child be once corrupted, let virtue be once disfigured or effaced in his soul, it will then be found most difficult afterwards to renew its image within him."

The Satiric Poet also, well knowing how easily children are scandalised, lays down the following maxim: "Maxima debetur puero reverentia—" the soul of the child should be held in the greatest reverence; because without this reverence people will not refrain from saying and doing things in the presence of children which must inevitably cause their innocence to be lost. It was but another way of putting the injunction of the Saviour—"Suffer the little children to come to Me;" for what those do who not having reverence for children scandalise and lead them into sin, is simply this—they prevent them from coming to Christ.

It is deserving of notice what reasons our Divine Lord assigns for the two-fold denunciation He utters—the one against those who scandalise children, and the other against those who prevent them from coming to Him; it is the same in both cases—namely, the dignity of the children; for in the former case He says—"Their angels see the face of their Father who is in heaven," and in the latter—"The kingdom of heaven is for such."

Let us now explain the nature of scandal, and the various ways in which it is given to the detriment and ruin of the souls of children.

Scandal is some exterior circumstance, generally something spoken or done, which gives rise to the injury or ruin of another's soul. He therefore is guilty of scandalising children who in any way does harm to their souls; who is the means of leading them into sin;

SECOND REFLECTION.

who is the culpable cause or occasion of their going aside from the path that conducts to Christ.

Scandal may be given in two ways—directly and indirectly.

As regards indirect scandal, he is guilty of it who does not prevent evil from accruing to another's soul, when he could and should prevent it; or, again, a person would be guilty of indirect scandal who, feeling himself called to the glorious work of aiding and rescuing human souls, should permit himself to be turned aside therefrom, either by the open censures or hidden calumnies of evil tongues, or by any of the other countless persecutions the spirit of wickedness may stir up against him.

The Apostles were guilty of the two kinds of scandal on the occasion before referred to; they were guilty of direct scandal when they strove to prevent the children from coming to Christ; they were guilty of indirect when they angrily rebuked the women who wished to bring them to Him.

How great their folly and blindness on this occasion was clearly shown by the feelings of indignation which their conduct aroused within the breast of the Saviour—"Whom when Jesus saw," says the Evangelist, "He was much displeased." Certainly that must have been highly reprehensible conduct on their part which could excite the anger of Him whose meekness and patience were so remarkable; which could disturb the serenity of Him who was the very fountain-head of all serenity and sweetness possible.

For the present moment I cannot recall any other incident in the Gospel which in the same way aroused the Saviour's indignation. With even such persons as publicans and sinners, notwithstanding all their crimes, He was the very essence of meekness and gentleness, and this despite the scornful protests of the self-righteous and hypocritical Pharasees, who were wont to taunt Him with his friendship and familiarty with this class of persons, saying to Him "Why do you eat with publicans and sinners?"

As for us Christians, let us carefully avoid all giving of scandal, direct and indirect, lest we bring down upon ourselves the anger of God, which, be it remembered, is infinitely more terrible than the anger of men.

That those who by direct and overt words or actions lead others into sin are guilty of scandal is evident to everyone. Yet there are many who do this; there are many who not merely indeed do evil in the presence of others, but who glory in the doing of it; who even, take pride in the most heinous enormities; who, animated by a spirit verily diabolical, try to get as many as they can to become sharers in their own iniquities, just as if the one thing they had at heart was that when lost themselves they should not be lost alone, but should have as many as possible going down with them into the abyss.

As Pagan Rome was not without her Cataline, so the Church of Christ is not without those who conspire against the well-being of her children; who mislead and corrupt them, and drag them into their own excesses.

SECOND REFLECTION.

So blinded are these unhappy men by the evil passions that devour them that they cease to be any longer under the influence of faith; and being delivered over to a sort of reprobate sense they indulge in those abominations mentioned by the Apostle in the Epistle to the Romans; nay, incredible as it may seem, in enormities still more execrable and hateful. Carried away by the fire of their evil desires they have no regard for the virtue either of stranger or of kindred; they spare not even the innocence and purity of childhood itself; no, everything must be spoiled, everything besmeared by the foulness of their detestable misdeeds. To such a depth does their licentiousness sometimes bring them down that what is right and what is wrong, that virtue and vice become all the same to them, neither being much better or worse than the other; so that we cannot regard Origen as being in any way in error when he declared that the only difference between a man possessed by a devil and a man inflamed by his wicked passion is, that the frenzy of the one is a misfortune for which he himself is not to blame, while that of the other must be imputed to him as his own abominable wickedness.

Can we be surprised then that in these our times much more than in any other "the thoughts and desires of man's heart should be prone to evil from his youth," seeing that children, who already possess within them the original corruption of human nature, are now-a-days made familiar with sin from their earliest years; are made to drink in the poison of it, as it were, from their very mothers' breasts?

In addition to all this, there are multitudes of parents and instructors who bestow little or no care on the morals of the children committed to their charge; the idea of diligently watching over them, of zealously disciplining and training them (duties to which they are strictly bound), being the last thing in the world that suggests itself to their minds.

And this being so, how can these poor children, thus left without an instructor or a guide, thus abandoned to their own unaided inexperience, surrounded too by a multiplicity of dangers, not to speak of their being for ever attended by a spirit of evil who unceasingly plots and labours for their destruction—under such circumstances as these, how can children do otherwise than most miserably fall away from innocence and virtue?

But would to God it were only from *neglect* that children had to suffer! What is far more deplorable still, they are in thousands of instances positively corrupted and ruined by the multitudes of scandals that are thrown in their way.

Evil deeds are done before their eyes; evil expressions and conversations are poured into their ears; improper pictures are exposed before their view; dangerous and impious hooks and periodicals are put into their hands—how with such pestiferous influences as these for ever assailing them can the children possibly be virtuous? how can they help being anything else but sinful and depraved?

SECOND REFLECTION.

The poetic satirist has declared that nothing so surely or so quickly corrupts the heart of man as *bad example given around the domestic hearth*, above all when that example proceeds from those who are placed in authority over us.

Experience proves the truth of this, for do we not invariably find that the son walks in the wicked footsteps of the father; that he does just what he sees his father doing before him?—"Like parent, like child," as the proverb expresses it.

And here we have the reason why there are so many evils now-a-days in society and the world for which there seems to be no remedy. For to remedy an evil the first thing necessary to be done is to *recognise* it; but now many things which are patently wicked and immoral are no longer regarded as such; they are, on the contrary, maintained to be innocent and lawful. "The immoral," as Seneca puts it, "has ceased to be immoral;" the vices have become virtues.

Scandals of this kind, treacherous, unsuspected scandals—evil impressed upon children as if it were good rather than evil—these are the most disastrous scandals of all. Woe unto those who are guilty of them, who by means of them prevent children from coming to their Saviour.

Bad as those are who give scandal openly and directly, it would be difficult to say if they are more to be reprobated than those who give it covertly and secretly.

Of this class are those men who, when others devote themselves in all sincerity to the important work of instructing and training children, will not leave them in peace, but must oppose them, hamper them, secretly plot against them, suggesting that all this interest they profess to take in children, all this labour undergone in their behalf, comes neither from piety nor zeal, but is all mere show and sham—all nothing but hypocrisy and pretence.

Now what is to be said of the individuals who are guilty of conduct such as this; what shall we say of their false and crafty method of acting? How shall we characterise it? Will it suffice to compare it to the cunning of the fox, or rather should we not liken it to that of the old serpent himself, who glides along smoothly and warily, who lies in ambush secretly, and who when occasion offers bites; with his deadly fangs?

Hard as it may be to counteract direct and overt scandal, it is much more difficult still to prevent the harm done by this covert scandal we speak of, just as it is much more difficult to contend against an enemy who is secret and hidden than against one who is open and declared.

Would that those who are guilty of it would reflect upon and take to heart a certain precept of the wise man. Did they do so they would soon learn to put a stop to their unworthy conduct. The precept is this—"Withhold not him from doing good who is able, if thou art able do good thyself also."

SECOND REFLECTION.

Oh! who will catch for us those little foxes that ravage the vineyard of the Lord, and that trample down the blooming garden of the Church? Secretly and slily do they creep in, betraying their presence in no way save by the traces they leave behind. And what traces are these? Flowers the most beautiful trampled down and destroyed; plants the most healthy and promising plucked up by the root; the work of the gardener frustrated and spoiled in a thousand ways.

How strange that men should lower themselves to this sly and underhand perpetration of so much mischief! What do they seek in it all? What advantage do they hope for? Rather what malice is it that has taken possession of their hearts and that makes them act as they do?

Some merely want to oppose the good done by others without being discovered opposing it; others are animated by a secret envy and jealousy at seeing their neighbour doing good which they are unwilling to do themselves; while others are so devoid of all piety and religion that when they witness anything of the kind in others they will not believe in it, but must endeavour to put it down as a certain ridiculous childishness and stupidity.

Alas! such is the world that, it abounds with scandals. But woe to the world because it is so; and woe especially to those who are the authors of the scandals; better for them that they should perish from the earth than that they should be the guilty cause of ruining so many souls, particularly the souls of children whom they prevent from coming to the Saviour.

THIRD REFLECTION.

Of the commendable zeal of those who conduct Children along the path which leads to Christ.

"He that causeth a sinner to be converted from the error of his ways shall save his soul from death, and shall cover a multitude of sins."

Saint Gregory, commenting on these words or the Apostle, draws from them the inference that of all the sacrifices which can be offered to the Almighty, that which is the most acceptable in His sight, is to labour for the salvation of souls.

If for the perishable things of time, if for the sake of those transitory goods which the Apostle reputes as loss rather than gain, men are so anxiously solicitous, if they strive and labour for them day and night, going at times to the length of exposing themselves to all sorts of dangers on their account, and if because they act in this way they are regarded as active, earnest, diligent men, and most useful members of society, what then is to be said of those who have no care, no zeal on behalf of the immortal souls of men, who experience no desire to promote the momentous interest of their eternal salvation; should not the sloth, the indifference, the evident want of faith of such persons be most severely censured and condemned; and is it not right that a much severer condemnation still should be visited upon those who oppose and strive to render futile the labours of well-meaning men, who endeavour to rescue souls from perdition, who do what they can to bring little children to Jesus Christ. Should a mere dumb beast fall into a trench or into the mire, everybody at once runs to its rescue, and no one will heed in the least whether the day be Sunday or holiday, or any other day; nor will it be suggested that in this there is anything at all reprehensible or wrong. Why then should censure be passed upon or fault found with one who gives his time and his labour to the glorious work of bringing souls to Christ—souls who frequently have such sore need of being brought to Him; souls buried in the mire of sin and groaning under the burthen of iniquities; souls enslaved by habits of vice and heavily weighted, perhaps by poverty and all its attendant inconveniencies and miseries?

The Holy Ghost by the mouth of Solomon enjoins upon us to do all we can for our neighbour, and to do it generously and willingly, "Whatsoever thy hand is able to do, do it earnestly," And again, "In the morning sow thy seed, and in the evening let not thy hand cease, for thou knowest not which may rather

THIRD REFLECTION.

spring up, this or that, and if both together, it shall be the better" (Eccl., ii., 6).

Miserable profligates in the world pay no heed to what others may say about them so long as they can indulge in their criminal delights, and shall the lover of Christ, the zealous worker for souls, be affrighted or turned aside from his course by every passing breath of censure, its if he were but some cowardly traveller who trembles at the shadow of every quivering reed? What! immortal souls, spiritual dwelling places of the Divinity, living temples and sanctuaries of the Holy Spirit, cities most sacred, kingdoms, which though yet on earth are truly celestial—these set on fire by hell around us, these being devoured and consumed by the various destructive human passions and vices; and we, shall we so fear the slanders of men or be so fast stuck in our own miserable sloth or indifference as not to be willing to run to their rescue?

A physician who gives his services to the sick gratuitously; an advocate who pleads for his clients without seeking remuneration; a workman who does his master's work and seeks no pay—such men are extolled to the stars for their unselfishness and generosity. Shall the spiritual physician then, the advocate of souls, the workman in the vineyard of the Lord—shall he meet only with censure and ridicule and opposition when he freely and heartily devotes himself to the salvation of the souls of children?

Where is the justice of this; does it look not rather like the most extravagant folly?

There are the poor children continually incited to evil by the pernicious lessons so incessantly given them, and must there be no one to oppose all this; no one to take the part of virtue; no one to unfold its charms before them so as to induce them to adopt and practice it. There are children hungry with the hunger of the spirit, crying for bread that can alone satisfy and nourish them; and is there to be no one to break it to them; or if those come forward who are willing to do so, must they meet with nothing but effronts and contradictions?

Surely all this is in direct opposition to the doctrine and example of Christ. Zeal, tender zeal, was what our Divine Saviour at all times practised. We know the striking and touching picture He made use of when He wished to describe His loving interest and tenderness towards the soul of men. He compared Himself to a hen gathering her chickens under her wings; to the creature which of all others, according to Saint Augustine, is the one most devoted and affectionate towards her young. "She spreads her wings," says the learned doctor, "she ruffles her feathers, she calls out in tender plaintive tones, and without having any care for herself or her own wants she attends only to those of her little brood; and should any enemy come upon the scene, oh! how stoutly and fiercely will she not fight for them, defending them to the very lost?

THIRD REFLECTION.

And we, who wish to be regarded us the followers and imitators of Christ, shall we have no zeal for souls, particularly the souls of children; shall we be without desire to do anything for them; or shall we work for them only fitfully and rarely, sometimes letting whole months pass by without making a single exertion in their behalf; Ah! may God forbid.

Various are the means whereby children can be brought into the way that conducts to Christ. One is Catechism, or public religious instruction; another, personal admonition and advice; a third, the school with its teaching and discipline.

But besides these there is a fourth (one that is altogether peculiar to the Christian religion), namely—Confession.

Whatever may be the opinion of others, I for my part frankly acknowledge, that I look upon Confession, *when it is all it ought to be*, as the most direct and effectual means for bringing children to Christ.

By confession the most hidden diseases of the soul are laid open, that is, when the confessor *adroitly and carefully examines* into everything; doing this with such *skill* as to draw forth the wriggling serpent from the soul and drive out the poisonous virus from the heart, for if this virus, this poison, be not ejected from the soul of the child it will never grow or expand in Christ; it will always remain languid and infirm, nay, it will continue to lie dead and buried in a very sink of vices and sins.

And how deplorable then the condition of the child: he performs no work of life, he makes no movement tending to bring him to the Saviour; the thorn being still rankling in his wound, his moral corruption becomes greater and greater day by day; and his conscience, while torn by the stings of a bitter and fruitless remorse, will, instead of bringing him repentance and peace, but toss him about in confusion and misery of mind, and make him daily more and more reckless in giving way to the many criminal desires which will not fail to spring up within his heart.

Moreover, as it is in confession that the disease of the soul is discovered and made known, so it is there the proper remedy for it is pointed out and applied.

And as to relapse—what better or more effectual means to prevent it can there be than confession?

But perhaps someone will say, Oh! yes, confession is very good for children, but there is no need for their going to it so very often, once, or at all events three or four times a year ought to be quite often enough.

Now we have given a sufficient answer to such an objection as this already when speaking of the great diligence and zeal displayed by people in the world when there is question of their merely temporal interests. If they think they never can do enough to advance these interests, which, after all are of no much consequence, why should there not be at least

THIRD REFLECTION.

a similar eagerness and zeal as regards the most precious interests of the souls of children; why should there not be as intense an anxiety about the adoption, the frequent adoption of a means so powerful for promoting these interests as confession most undoubtedly is, though in saying this we are far from wishing to exaggerate or to counsel a frequency of confession which would be imprudent or excessive.

Would to God that all children made every year even *one good integral and satisfactory* confession!

But since the number of children is everywhere great, and since the paschal season is so short that confessors can scarcely find the time to examine carefully and minutely into consciences, it is *expedient*, nay, it is *necessary*, for every child to make at some convenient time a *general confession* of the sins of his life *to some wise and prudent confessor*, doing this not hurriedly or by halves but seriously, *leisurely and carefully*.

There are three very good reasons why children should make stick a confession.

The first is this. *Multitudes of children* seduced by their own passion or by the wickedness of others *fall into very heinous sins, which they do not know how or have not the courage to confess*. Now, in the confession we speak of they can be induced to acknowledge these sins if only they are duly *instructed*, *admonished* and *interrogated*; and having confessed them they can then be properly enlightened as to the malice that is in them, care being taken, however, not to give them a knowledge of evil that would be if prejudice to their souls, or should it so happen that they come to know, through confession, of sin which they did not know before, they should forthwith be inspired with such a dread and abhorrence of it as will afterwards secure them against the misfortune of committing it. Thus the sins being fully confessed, and the malice of them being duly appreciated and deplored, the children will obtain for them a full and entire remission.

Another advantage of such a confession is that the children will henceforth know what sins they ought to confess, and in what manner they ought to confess them, besides which they will have the benefit of receiving on occasion of making this confession *most effective counsel and advice never*, on any account during their future lives, *to disguise or conceal anything in their confessions.*

There is a third advantage also. It may happen that these children adverting in after life to their former sins will conceive certain troublesome scruples about them, and begin to think they must go over the confession of them again, a thing which would be much more difficult for them now, which would cause them much more confusion and shame, than in the simple and ingenuous days of childhood. But since they have made this general confession we speak of, their confessor can easily set their minds

THIRD REFLECTION.

at rest by assuring them that they have already fully complied with the obligation of confession, and they need not now or at any other time subject themselves to the ordeal of again declaring these former sins.

No one will consider these three advantages of trifling importance, who knows what a *fearful tyranny false shame is capable of exercising* over some souls, the more particularly when they have been *guilty of certain heinous sins* which are of their nature shameful, which are shameful and abominable even in the estimation of those guilty of them, which have had the effect of degrading and debasing not merely their bodies, but even their very minds as well.

Whosoever has been able to gather experience in this respect will, I think, acknowledge that it is almost as difficult to induce people of this kind to acknowledge their sins as it would be to cause a perpetually dumb person to speak.

Perhaps it will be said to me, or to persons like me who are very much engaged in the work of instructing the young or hearing their confessions—it is no use what you do for these children; you are but wasting your time with them; they will not confess their sins to you; they will only tell you lies about them, and disguise them; or if they do acknowledge them what good in it all since they will immediately fall back into the same sins again.

Now let us make answer to the last part of this objection first. Children, it is said, will relapse into their sins. They may indeed relapse; but do not others who are no longer children, do not even grown persons relapse; yet we do not see them for this reason giving up confession. Does the sailor discontinue pumping the water out of the hold of his ship because after a while some more water has leaked in again? "We fight against vices," says Seneca, "not that we may get entirely rid of them, but that we may not become their slaves," And we wash our hands, not because they are clean, but because they are soiled; and because we know the oftener we wash them the cleaner they will be, and the less liable to have new defilements cling to them.

I know very well children are apt sometimes to conceal their sins (do grown people never do so?) especially when they first begin to make their confessions. But even so, the truth can be got from them by little and little, if they are only *taken gently and kindly, and carefully and skilfully examined.* Or should they be unwilling to confess their sins at present, they will do so later on, when the fear of God shall have been developed in them and taken full possession of their hearts.

No doubt there may be a few, whom, as the Scripture says, "God has despised," and whom on that account "no one can correct;" nevertheless there will be always many who can be brought to confess and amend; and indeed were it only one in a month, or one in a year, that a zealous worker had thus rescued and saved, his labour would not by any means have been in vain; for we know the consoling truth of which the Holy Ghost assures us—"Charity covereth a multitude of sins."

THIRD REFLECTION.

Wherefore let every one, who (like myself) can look back upon sins of his own, whether in childhood or in later years, enkindle within his soul an ardent zeal for this glorious work of "covering" the sins of others; of *covering* them, that is, bringing about their forgiveness; let him exert himself to the utmost to "convert the sinner from the error of his way and to deliver his soul from death."

And you above all, masters, teachers, rectors—you to whose care communities of children have been entrusted—watch over your charge and keep them in the strictest discipline (and this I say to you in all simplicity and brotherly charity, and not as wanting to act the master towards you, or as having any doubts that you do not herein discharge your duty), and not merely never do anything or permit anything that would prevent those young souls from coming to Christ, but on the contrary do everything you possibly can to bring them to Him.

And since there is no class of persons among whom moral evil is so likely to be mutually contagious as among the young, let it be your care to use the utmost vigilance so as to discover the depraved, the infected ones among your pupils. "One tainted sheep," as the proverb says, "is enough to infect the entire flock;" even so, one corrupt youth is sufficient to contaminate many, even of the good among his,' or her companions. "With the perverse thou wilt be perverted" is the statement and warning of the

Prophet (Ps, xvii., 27). And again, "They were mingled with the heathens, and learned their works, and served their idols, and it became a stumbling-block to them" (cv. 35)

You know how you would act if you were conscious that certain acts of theft, even trifling ones, were being committed by some one under your care; you would go to much trouble to discover the delinquent; and when you had discovered him you would severely reprove him; perhaps you would even go so far as to expel him from the society of his companions. But you should remember that there is another kind of theft which is much more criminal and harmful still than that of material things—a theft that may be justly accounted a species of sacrilege; it is robbing children of their innocence; violating, defiling, destroying the sacred temple of their souls. Against this sort of thievery you ought to be immeasurably more vigilant and more strict than against the other; and if it be out of your power to discover and to punish all who are guilty of it, at least you ought to make sure that whenever any culprit succeeds in escaping detection it will not be owing to any want of care or vigilance on your part.

But, perhaps, you will say—Oh! there are no culprits of this kind among those under my charge; or if there be, certainly I am not aware of it.

Would that there were none; would that there were only a few! It is to be feared, however, that if you

THIRD REFLECTION.

only opened your eyes and looked into things somewhat more closely and carefully you would find there was good reason for thinking differently from what you do.

If upon discovering a guilty party you publicly and severely chastise him, the chastisement may be very painful to the individual concerned, but it will be sure to act as a salutary deterrent on a number of others; and this especially where there is question of an offence in that matter which modesty prevents us from naming.

Possibly your severity may have the effect of causing a few to withdraw themselves from under your authority, on the plea that you are too severe, and your discipline too exacting; even so, you will not thereby be a loser; a kind providence will look well to the interests of your school or your institute, and will bring you more numerous and more creditable pupils than those you have lost—pupils, who will be attracted as well by the regularity and discipline of the place as by the virtue and good conduct of its inmates; for after all nothing is more lovable, and nothing has greater power to attract to itself, than genuine Christian virtue and goodness.

Finally let us be permitted to admonish all without exception to watch over their conduct and intercourse with children, so that no one amongst those little ones of Christ may ever have to reproach them in the words of the prophet—"In this way wherein I walked, they have hidden a snare for me" (Ps. cxli., 4); or again—"They have laid for me a stumbling-block by the way-side (Ps, cxxxix., 6).

Such a snare, such a stumbling-block would to anything whatever, that either directly or indirectly, either in regard of the children themselves or those who work for them, would be a hindrance to the fulfilment of the words of the Saviour—"Suffer the little children, and forbid them not to come to Me."

FOURTH REFLECTION.

An apologetic for our own ministry in regard of Children, together with an appeal to them to come to Christ through the medium of that ministry humble though it be.

"IF A MAN BE overtaken in any fault, you who are spiritual instruct such, a one in the spirit of meekness, considering thyself lest thou also be tempted" (Gal., vi., 1).

No small knowledge certainly of human nature did that man possess who was the originator of the saying—"The art of arts is that of governing souls."

Sublime and difficult as this art is, nevertheless many persons presume to undertake it, though but very indifferently qualified for the task. Hence it is we have such frequent verification of the word of sacred Scripture—"The blind leading the blind;" hence also have we so many spiritual and moral evils menacing us on every side.

So little is the sublimity, the grandeur, of this work of disciplining and moulding souls understood, that if a person of mark, such, for instance, as a theologian or a man of letters, devote himself to it, especially in regard of children, he is at once looked upon as having abandoned his proper place and calling, and as having done something foolish and ridiculous (a verdict which some people have thought well to pass upon myself).

It was into an error of this kind that the Apostles fell on the occasion of their turning away the women who wished to present their children to our Lord; for being as yet very imperfectly skilled in heavenly things they judged it unworthy of so great a Master and Doctor that He should give His care and concern to such insignificant beings as little children. This mistake, however, He was quick to point out to them, as well by the words He made use of as by His manner of acting towards the children—"Suffer, He cried out, "Suffer the little children to come to Me;" and then, as the Evangelist narrates, *embracing* them, and *laying hands upon them He blessed them*."

The important lesson conveyed to us in all this by our Divine Lord is confirmed by the words of Saint Paul quoted above. Those who would be instructors of others, says the Apostle, should be *spiritual* men, and should possess a spirit of gentleness and condescension; and they ought never to lose sight of their own infirmity and misery so that they may at all times be disposed to have due consideration and commiseration for the infirmity and misery of others.

But truly spiritual men, how rare they are!

FOURTH REFLECTION.

Who it will be asked is the *spiritual* man. The spiritual man is he who judges things according to the spirit; who has learned from what he himself has suffered to feel for the sufferings of others; who is, solicitous, not for the things that are his own, but for these that are Jesus Christ's; who has his heart so replenished with Christian charity, humility and piety, that there can no longer be found room in it for miserable vanity and self-seeking; "whose conversation is in heaven;" who like one of God's angels is affected neither by words of praise or censure; who imitating the guardian spirits of men never allows the lowliness of his occupation to bring down his mind from the apprehension of things divine; who, while he heals the moral infirmities of others, takes care to preserve his own soul from contagion (being ever mindful of the warning of the Saviour, that it "profiteth a man nothing to gain the whole world should he lose his soul," and never losing sight also of the injunction of the Wise Man—"Have pity on thy own soul pleasing God").

Finally, the spiritual man is one who never permits himself to be drawn away or allured by the outward attractions of creatures, but guided at all times by the clear light of reason takes account only of souls, of their sanctification and salvation.

Should these qualities be wanting in you, should you be easily disturbed by the opinions of men, easily put about by what they say or do against you, should you be readily puffed up by success or cast down by failure—you are then not a spiritual but a carnal man, and accordingly unsuited for the heavenly work of instructing others in the spirit of meekness.

These things being so (to go back to what I was saying about myself), I consider it more just that I should be censured for my temerity in undertaking the instruction of children than that I should be reproached with having thereby lowered my dignity and self-respect; for in undertaking such an occupation what have I done only made bold to enrol myself among the number of the spiritual, compared with whom I know very well I am but as the crawling tortoise to the birds that soar.

But then what am I to do? Some tell me,—even good and well-meaning men maintain it—that this is not at all the kind of work I should be engaged in. And they allege various reasons for this, particularly the four following:—

They say that my habits and ways are utterly different from those of the children, and that consequently I am unsuited to be their instructor. They allege that occupying the eminent position I do I ought to engage myself in works of a more honourable and exalted nature. Then they find fault with me as regards the circumstances of time and place in connection with my work for children. Finally they say that this line of conduct I have taken up is a singularity and an innovation, and cannot but give rise to very

FOURTH REFLECTION.

inconvenient criticisms and calumnies. Let us make a few remarks by way of reply to these allegations.

They say there is a great disparity between me and the children, between my habits of mind and theirs. This is certainly true. But why should I on that account be unable to render myself useful to them? Why cannot I accommodate my ways to theirs? Why cannot I bring myself down to their level? And if I but do this what is to prevent me from being of very great benefit to them?

Certainly one must condescend much to children, if he is to do them good. "Pride and love," the poet says, "do not agree well together, and they will not be long found sitting side by side." If you hold yourself too high for children, *if you do not condescend to them in all meekness and humility, and thus draw to yourself the affections of their young hearts*, you may indeed endeavour to instruct them, but *your instructions will be of no avail*, they will not care to listen to them, and still less will they care to put them in practice.

Wherefore if you would be of any use to children you must lay aside all haughtiness and sternness of manner; *you must make yourself a child for the children's sake*; you must put on their methods and ways, always excepting of course, their vices and defects, and more particularly everything, whether in look or word or gesture, that could in the least degree be out of harmony with the strictest purity and modesty.

"Human nature," says Seneca, "always so prone to rebel is much more easily *led* than driven; you will get good of it much better by *gentleness* than by sternness. And it has often been remarked that those of a generous and ingenuous nature (and this is true of animals no less than men) have this peculiarity about them, that they are much more powerfully influenced by caresses than by threats, that gentle methods have much more influence over them than those that are harsh and severe—considerations which if duly reflected on cannot but convince us what our manner of dealing with children ought to be.

Moreover, how will children, who are naturally so excessively timid and bashful, *be able to confess their sins*, their indelicate sins especially, *to him whom they have learned to dislike or perhaps to dread?* or how will they confess them even to one *who has not by his mildness and affability convinced them that he is their true, devoted, and affectionate friend?*

But by what means will he be able to convince them that he is such a friend? By a spirit of condescension towards them, by showing himself pleased when they are pleased, by manifesting an interest in all their concerns, even their recreations and amusements, by rejoicing with them when they have gained any little innocent or creditable success, such, for instance, as in the matter of their studies, by avoiding all harshness and bitterness towards them even when administering to them necessary

FOURTH REFLECTION.

correction, *by treating them habitually in a gentle and kindly manner,* thus making them feel, not merely that one has no dislike of them and is in no way estranged from them, but on the contrary that the *sentiment one entertains towards them is that of a sincere and affectionate regard.*

If one does not comport oneself in this way towards children, *if by his manner of treating with them he does not make himself pleasing and agreeable to them,* the inevitable consequence will be that *all the instructions and admonitions he gives them will be entirely fruitless;* and should he be a priest they certainly *will not make their confessions to him as they ought.*

I am confident that the Apostle Saint Paul did not adopt any ether method than this in his dealings with children, for how could he have said that he made himself all things to all men to gain all to Christ, if he made an exception of children, if he did not *make himself a child* in order to gain them? And what right would he have to insist upon parents being gentle and kind towards their children, and on their "not provoking them to indignation lest they be discouraged," if he himself acted in a different manner, if he was cold and unkind to them, or kept aloof from them as being unworthy of his notice or of his society?

But, after all, what need is there I should go on reasoning in this way about the action of the Apostle since we have his own express declaration that this and no other was his method—"But we became little ones," he says, "in the midst of you, as if a nurse should cherish her children?" (Thess. ii., 7).

Let us revert once more to the reasons the Apostle had for asserting that when we instruct those taken in any fault we ought to do so in a spirit of meekness; and let us at the same time see if our Lord does not, both by word and example, entirely agree in this matter with the thoughts and sentiments of the Apostle.

"Come to me," said the Saviour on a certain occasion, "all you that labour and are burthened." He invited all to come to Him. But how were they to come unless encouragement was given to them to do so, unless He Himself made the way more or less easy for them? But He did make it easy for them. How? By the gentleness and approachableness of His character; for was He not, as He Himself declared, *meek and humble of heart*?

In the lives of the ancient Fathers there are many incidents recorded, which go to prove what we are maintaining—viz., that nothing has greater power to induce people to rectify and amend their lives than meekness and gentleness—a truth, which even the heathen poet seems to indicate when he says—"The best and most useful thing man possesses is his gentleness, his meekness."

It is narrated of Saint John, that divinely favoured Apostle, who was so wonderfully enlightened as to heavenly things, and who was able to

FOURTH REFLECTION.

write about them in so admirable a manner, that he did not think it beneath him to go so far as to kiss the hand of a most abandoned robber and murderer thereby to win him to God and His divine service.

And how was Saint Augustine gained over to the Church in which he afterwards became so shining a light, so eminent and, useful a doctor? By the meekness and charity of Saint Ambrose, "I began," says the Saint, speaking of Ambrose, "I began to love the man, not because he taught me the truth, but because he was kind to me," O most prudent Ambrose, man guided by the spirit of God! he did not, when encountering Augustine, puffed up as he then was with pride and his erroneous doctrines, turn upon him angrily and harshly, and tell him to begone from him, that he was a sinner, a heretic, a blasphemer; nothing at all of the kind. And if he did not treat the heretical Augustine in this way, how much farther would he have, been from conducting himself with harshness or asperity towards the little children of the one true Church, the tender lambs of the fold of the Saviour?

Furthermore, since every act of Christ is not without its meaning, since it is in itself a lesson, we may be certain that when He invited the children to come to Him, and when He reproved the Apostles for trying to prevent them, and when on their coming nigh He "laid hands upon them, embraced them, and blessed them," it was His intention in all this to convey to mankind a salutary and important lesson, as to what their manner of dealing with children ought to be.

Who then, O most loving Jesus, will hesitate or be ashamed to make himself little for the sake of children? Who will be so elated with a sense of his own importance, or so puffed up with his learning and wisdom, as to look down upon and despise those little ones because of their littleness, their weakness or ignorance, seeing that Thou, who art the Lord God, "blessed for ever, in whom are hid all the treasures of wisdom and knowledge," hast deigned in the excess of Thy goodness to stretch forth Thy sacred arms towards them and enfold them in Thy most pure embraces?

Far then from us be everything like haughtiness and undue severity of manner towards children, which can only have the effect of repelling them from us and making them lose their confidence in us.

This example of our Blessed Lord embracing and caressing children by far exceeds the admirable condescension of Socrates (so highly eulogised by the philosophers themselves), who, after discharging public functions of the highest importance, was accustomed to relax his mind by taking part in the amusements of children, even in such as were quite simple and puerile, not deeming that in all this he was doing anything in any way derogatory of his dignity or station. O, if the censorious Catos of the present day could have seen him on such occasions how would they not have laughed at him, and what fine derision would they not have heaped upon him!

FOURTH REFLECTION.

In making these remarks we are far from counselling any intercourse with children which would be wanting in that strict reserve and decorum that it is always necessary to observe in our relations with them. Nevertheless to condescend to them, even so far as to participate in their games and amusements, is not merely harmless, it may even be of considerable utility to us. To say the least of it it is an innocent recreation for the mind; and besides it is a very excellent means of humbling ourselves before God, and thereby rendering to Him a certain most acceptable homage and reverence, not unlike to that which holy David rendered, when, divesting himself of his royal robes so as to appear vile in his own eyes, he danced with all his might before the ark.

This last is the very best motive one can have in his actions; and it is a motive with which one can scarcely go too far.

Moreover, does not the humbling of oneself in this way seem perfectly in keeping with the salutary injunction of Ecclesiasticus, which Cicero does not hesitate to adopt in his *De Officiis*—"The greater thou art, the more humble thyself in all things" (iii., 20)?

And is it not also very much in harmony with the lesson taught by Our Lord, when, taking a child, He placed it before His disciples and said to them—"He that is lesser among you, he is the greater" (Luke, ix., 46); and again when ho said—"Amen I say to you, whosoever shall not receive the kingdom of God as a little child, shall not enter it" (Mark, xvi., 16).

I aver before God, in whose presence I dare state only what is true, that during the three years I have been ministering to children I have met with many, some even pretty well advanced in age, who have acknowledged to me that they *never would have confessed their sins to any one*, unless to somebody who, like me, would have been *excessively kind* to them and would *have interrogated and helped them*; that they would not have confessed them *though they were dying and knew they would have been damned for not doing so.*

See then what gentleness and condescension can effect for children; see especially what a salutary work you can as confessor operate upon them if you but carefully *admonish and interrogate* them, and strive to *manage them* generally with a *certain skilful prudence and tact*; or rather see what God Himself will be sure to accomplish in them through means of your ministry, if while you honestly labour for them you also humbly and confidently pray for His divine assistance, thereby bringing down his salutary blessing on all you do in their behalf.

Furthermore, I have heard it stated by men of many years experience in hearing the confessions of children, that they seldom or never *had met with any one addicted to certain vices who had previously confessed them to any priest*; and they moreover declared they would not have confessed these vices even to themselves had they not treated them with the *greatest gentleness and prudence*, and even taken

FOURTH REFLECTION.

the precaution of *circumventing them by certain pious manœuvres and stratagems.*

Let me now reply somewhat briefly to the three other points alleged against me; for as to what is said in reference to my position and the dignity of my office I think I need not say anything more, having already given a sufficient answer on this head.

They contend that I ought to engage myself in occupations of a more exalted and important character.

For my part I do not know of anything of greater importance to which my weakness could devote itself than to rescue from the claws of the devil and from the gulf of hell the souls of children—those dear little ones who constitute such a precious portion of the Church—than to plant, as it were, and water those tender saplings, so that the Almighty, shedding down upon them the divine influence of His grace, may bestow upon them a heavenly increase.

But they say, I can do so much more splendid work by sermons and discourses in the public churches.

More *splendid* work, I dare say, *but not work more salutary or more fruitful.* This desire after all of preaching to large congregations need not necessarily proceed from a very pure motive; it may arise possibly from pride and vanity. Our Divine Lord at all events teaches us by His own example to moderate and restrain such a desire, for do we not read of Him in the Gospel as holding a very prolonged discourse with *one* single soul for the purpose of doing her spiritual good—viz., the Samaritan Woman?

I confess indeed I should be acting very unwisely, if for the sake of my work for children or any good that might follow therefrom, I were neglecting my own special duties as Chancellor of the University; but when I have seen to and honestly discharged these duties, and when, as not unfrequently happens, I happen to have some leisure hours on my hands, who will say I am not free to give these hours to a work so holy and so salutary; why the truth is, if I spent this my free time in something immeasurably less useful, if I spent it merely in innocent amusement or legitimate, recreation, no one would think of suggesting that I was doing anything reprehensible or wrong.

And as regards the unseasonableness of the time and place of my work for children, which is the third charge lodged against me, I have already in a former reflection made somewhat of a reply to this; here, however, I may remark, that the place where I carry on my work for children is the public church, which certainly is the most suitable place that can be found, and which is the most likely of all others to banish unfair suspicions from the minds of the uncharitable. It is only the person who does evil, as our Saviour says, "who shuns the light;" we who are conscious to ourselves of doing not evil but good rather court the light and seek it; and all the more

FOURTH REFLECTION.

readily as we remember the precept which has been laid upon us of "letting the light of our good works shine before men," and of "putting our candle not under a bushel" where nobody can see it, but "on the candlestick where it may give light to all."

Notwithstanding all this there are those who put an evil interpretation on our conduct and take scandal at it, saying that it is all vanity and show and pretence or worse.

Well, if they act in this way it is their own affair. What reason have they got to take scandal as they do? None whatever. Their's is scandal taken, but not given; their's is Pharasaical scandal which we may very well disregard and despise, seeing that there is nothing whatever in our action or in the circumstances attending it that can with the least shadow of reason be construed into a bad or mischievous example for the faithful.

It is not at all a matter of surprise to us that there should be persons who view things in this uncharitable and perverse fashion, no more than it would be to us a subject of wonder that the ray of light, which is so pleasant to eyes that are sound and healthy, should be painful and distressing to those that are diseased and sore. "We are the good odour of Christ," the Apostle declares; but observe what he adds, while we are "an odour of life unto life to some," we are "*an odour of death unto death to others.*"

Instead of raising objections about time and place in regard of this important work of the salvation of souls, I believe that anyone who considers well how ripe and how abundant everywhere is the harvest to be gathered, and how few the workmen to gather it (I mean *really efficient* workmen, for those of another sort, those who, to use the language of Horace, seem disposed rather to "consume the fruits of the harvest than to labour to save it," are numerous enough)—I believe that such a one will easily be convinced that there is no place, no day, no hour, that ought to be excluded from this glorious work.

Finally, as regards the fourth charge alleged against me—that my conduct is novel, eccentric, and without precedent—I grant that my predecessors did not engage themselves in this sort of work; but then here the familiar old proverb comes to my rescue—"Everyone according to his taste."

And what objection is it to a work to say that it is new or unusual? New things must be undertaken at times, without them society could not possibly subsist, it should indeed necessarily collapse and go to pieces altogether.

But really is what I do so new or extraordinary? Do we not every other day see workmen going forth to the harvest of the Lord, some to labour in this way and some in that, all of them being duly commissioned thereto by those who have charge of the harvest—namely, bishops and superiors? I am merely one of these workmen.

FOURTH REFLECTION.

If it be further objected to me that it was of my own motion I sought permission to give myself to this work, I answer—what of that; have I not the word of the Saviour to justify me: "Pray ye the Lord of the harvest that he send forth labourers into his harvest" (Matt., ix., 38); and do we not read in Isaias, that when the Almighty spoke and said—"Whom shall I send, and who shall go for us," the prophet immediately replied—"Lo, here am I, send me."

I entirely fail to see what can be wrong or out of order in this conduct of mine, the more especially as I have the sanction of my superiors for it, and since I never allow myself to undertake the instruction or guidance of any children without first acquainting those who have a right to know who it is that instructs and confesses them.

Finally, having been appointed Chancellor of the Church of Paris, and being charged in no small measure both by my office and by Apostolic mandate with the care of schools and pupils, I do not know anything more in harmony with my position or the duties it imposes than to exert myself according to my knowledge and ability to promote the moral and religious formation of the young.

My very friends, it may be, will take up the objections of others against me, and say—O your opponents, you must know, will put down this unusual method of action on your part to eccentricity, to singularity, to childishness, or some such thing.

Ah! my most dear friends, I know very well what my opponents will say; I have foreseen it long and have been well prepared for it. For what man was there ever yet occupying a position of prominence whose actions have not been found fault with, and even viciously and stupidly maligned?

At the same time this I ask—and I ask it in the name of that salvation to which we all aspire, and in the presence of that God before whose judgment-seat we must one day appear—that (since "no one knoweth the things that are within a man save the spirit of a man himself") no one will judge me save according to the standard laid down by Christ—that is, "by my works." If my works are evil, if there is anything immoral in what I do, anything unsound in what I teach, then let me be adjudged—and I submit to the judgment—as nothing else than a wolf in sheep's clothing.

But if this is not so, if on the contrary my works are good, then let no one put me down as having an evil intent in doing them. He who would thus rashly judge and condemn me not only sins against the charity lie owes his brother, but he is guilty also of placing a scandal in the way of children, who by such things are not unfrequently prevented from coming to the Saviour.

On the great day of trial that is coming all unjust and uncharitable censors shall have to render a rigid account of their conduct, but as for me I shall in that hour stand free in so far at all events as my

FOURTH REFLECTION.

engaging in this work for children is concerned. This my conscience testifies to me, and my perfect peace of soul as reflected in my exterior may give a similar testimony to those who know me; and if other witnesses still be wanting I have them in those multitudes of children for whom I have been labouring, and whose frank and ingenuous nature will make them ready to tell the truth about me even to my disadvantage, should there be anything of the kind to be disclosed.

And now having said so much to others let me turn to the children themselves, and have a word with them.

And I will begin by appealing to them in the words of the Book of Wisdom—"Whosoever is a little one let him come to me," and let him come without being in the least timid or afraid. No matter who the child may be, let him come and hear were it only some few simple words of counsel from my lips. This appeal I hesitate not to make; for I have a right to make it, not of myself, no, but in Christ Jesus.

My one endeavour with regard to every child who comes to me will be to urge on to whatever is right and good, and among other things it wilt be my care to counsel him to recount the years of his life in the bitterness of his soul (Isaias, xxxviii., 15), and "to sweep his spirit," so to say, with the brush of his own tongue—that is I will exhort him to make at some period of his childhood a general confession of his life; but neither this nor anything else shall I at any time try to force on anybody against his will.

Moreover, in my dealings with children I shall be careful never to put to them useless or irrelevant questions; nor shall I permit them, on their part to make known to me things regarding their companions or anyone else which it would be better and wiser not to disclose.

As to the seal of confession, let no one ever dream I could in the least infringe against it, I am fully conscious how strict, how sacred this seal is.

And I could very earnestly desire that my penitents would be as circumspect in regard to what passes in confession as I am myself, and that they would never permit a foolish and wicked curiosity on the part of others to extract from them those holy confidences, which taking place in the secrecy of the sacred tribunal, had better been kept for God's knowledge only.

Possibly some one may be deterred from coming to confession lest I should impose upon him a penance too difficult and severe.

No need to be afraid of this. Like William of Paris I much prefer to send souls to purgatory with a small and easy penance which they will be sure to perform, than to send them to hell with a, long and difficult one which they will culpably omit.

Whoever comes to me let his sins be what they may, yet if he but confesses them frankly and

FOURTH REFLECTION.

honestly, omitting nothing, and at the same time cries out like David from the depths of a repentant heart, "I have sinned against the Lord," I for my part shall be only too glad to say to him at once, as Nathan said to his royal penitent—"The Lord hath taken away thy sin," I confess I never could regard as by any means the least important element in true repentance that disgust and abhorrence of sin which drives the sinner almost perforce to confession, there honestly to acknowledge his sin and vomit it forth, as it were, out of his soul.

I do not know there can be anyone so foolish as to imagine that should he come to me to confession I would afterwards entertain towards him feelings of disdain and dislike. Never could I do anything of the kind. On the contrary no matter who the penitent be who comes to me, I shall always cherish him as my most dear child in Christ Jesus; I shall regard him as one who now possesses the fear of the Almighty, who is washed white and pure in His divine sight. And what will tend to make my esteem and regard for him all the greater will he the remembrance of the touching confidence he reposed in me when he came and laid open to me wounds and sores which he could never have the courage to disclose even to his nearest and dearest relatives.

In such manner in truth am I affected interiorly towards penitents that the more heinous be the sins I see them repentant of the greater is the sympathy I have for them, and the more tender is the gentleness with which I feel disposed to treat them; and I am certain that were I to encounter some poor soul who had been guilty of the most horrible enormity—say the murder of his own parents—even towards such a one I would never permit myself to entertain the slightest feeling of hatred or resentment.

I am aware that penitents usually experience a certain sentiment of awkwardness or shyness in the presence of him to whom they have confessed their sins; though indeed it would be better this were not the case. Such a feeling however soon dies away, and even while it lasts it need not be altogether useless, it can be turned to one's spiritual account by being humbly accepted as an atonement for former sins.

But perhaps some one loth to come to confession will say—Oh! I am but a cold and indevout sort of soul; I do not care for confession, nor do I see what good it is going to do me.

Now, granted that you are cold and have no devotion, I say for this very reason you ought to make use of confession, for it is there you will have spoken to you that "kindling word of God" which will not fail to dissipate your coldness and excite within you the spirit of fervour. How often have I not seen persons coming to the sacrament carelessly and indifferently, or it might be utterly against their will; at all events not believing it would do them any good; yet they have gone away from it entirely different—they

FOURTH REFLECTION.

have gone away penitent and consoled, sometimes even shedding abundance of tears.

Interior impressions and transformations of this kind we have all of us from time to time experienced. The following is a case in point with regard to myself:—

Some considerable time since I was recommending two sisters under my direction to adopt the virginal method of life, my piety suggesting to me that it was by this they would best please the Almighty, and most securely advance the interests of their own souls. After some time, however, doubts and anxieties began to take possession of my mind; this kind of life was so exceptional, the custom of the world was so entirely opposed to it. Discomposed and discouraged by these ideas I had almost abandoned my purpose and was on the point of giving a contrary advice to these two persons, when, by God's mercy, raising my thoughts from earth to heaven, from time to eternity, from this present death to the life to come, and remembering in the light of reason and of faith that all things here below are but "vanity and vanity of vanities," I was immediately enlightened and strengthened, and once for all firmly established in the purpose my piety had at first suggested to me.

Where is the human soul that has not at times as great, or it may be much greater, need than I on this occasion of being enlightened and sustained, of being encouraged to follow, not what the custom of the crowd approves, or what their own ideas for the moment imagine to be right, but what is in accordance with the unerring principles of faith and right reason? For my part I do not know any place where this enlightenment can be more certainly or more effectively given than *in confession*.

When instructing my penitents, my custom is (and this I must not hesitate to mention) to exhort them to do four things in particular.

But first I may also state that I am wont to endeavour to inspire my penitents with a special horror of certain kinds of sin—viz., the four following:—perjury and falsehood; detraction and calumny; injustice and violence; and lastly, impurity in action, above all those forms of it which are so gross and heinous that they are condemned even by the civil law itself.

And now with regard to the four things I require my penitents to do. First of all I ask them *never on any account to cause sin or spiritual ruin to another*, this being a work fit only for the devil himself. (There is wisdom surely in the civil enactment, which requires that if a man will not be pure he will at least not be scandalous; that if he must be immoral he will not at all events parade his immorality to the contamination and perversion of his neighbours).

Secondly, I try to secure of my penitents that they exert themselves, in all prudence of course, to bring back

FOURTH REFLECTION.

to virtue those whom they have formerly led astray, or who have been accomplices of their guilt; that they even try to make compensation for the evil they have done in the past by drawing other souls also from vice in this way doing no longer in the world the work of demons, but fulfilling instead the charitable offices of angels.

Thirdly, I ask of them that should they relapse into sin (for human, frailty is very great), they *have recourse again to confession* as their main resource and hope; than which, however, there is nothing less to be desired, nothing more harmful (and this I *repeatedly try to impress* upon their minds), unless they make it *sincerely* and well, unless they *honestly and sufficiently* confess their sins, with the number of them and the *necessary circumstances*, above all those circumstances which change the species.

Fourthly, I assign to them, not as a matter of obligation, but of counsel merely, some rather easy practice of devotion, which they are continually to adhere to, and which when thus kept up will be to them a perpetual reminder of their sins, which will constitute an excellent atonement for them; and which likewise will be a very good means of preventing them from falling back into them again.

The practice I generally assign is the recital morning and evening of a "Pater" and "Ave" (with perhaps a prostration on the ground when such might be deemed advisable).

I seldom or never appoint a practice different from this, no matter what be the character of the penitents with whom I have to deal, partly because it would be scarcely practicable to do so, and partly because appointing a variety of penitential practices to any one would be only too likely to give rise to troubles and scruples of conscience. And if in enjoining this identical practice on all I am no more severe on those who come burthened with many sins than on those who have but little on their conscience, these latter can scarcely with, justice complain, since they are not less bounden to Almighty God than the others, seeing that, though they have not, like them, fallen into great and numerous sins, they owe this signal favour to the divine goodness which has in a special way most mercifully supported and protected them.

In conclusion, dear children, permit me to address you in the words of the Holy Spirit—"How long, O Children, will you love childishness" (Prov. i., 22); or again—"Why do you love vanity and seek after lying" (Psal. iv., 3). Be no longer silly or foolishly afraid; come to me; and come with confidence; there is "no snare set for you in the way," no "serpent lying hid for you in the grass;" come and we shall communicate our goods mutually to one another—our *spiritual* goods of course, for there is no question of temporal ones. I on my side will impart to you the light of holy doctrine, and you on yours will give to me the benefit of your pious prayers; not only so, but I will not fail

FOURTH REFLECTION.

to offer up prayers for you as you for me; and thus we shall advance for each other the supreme interest of our sanctification and salvation to the intense joy of our dear Guardian Angels, on whose feast, as it happens, I am penning to you these words.

And so perhaps it may be, so indeed it shall be, that we will find grace and favour with our heavenly Father, provided always we continue obedient to His voice—I in pointing out to you how you are to please Him and attain to Him, and you in faithfully following the lessons which by His grace I have the privilege of imparting to you.

Nor shall consolations be wanting to us meantime during the course of our pilgrimage here below; the grace of God, His love, our union with Him—these will be our daily joy and comfort; and when eternity arrives we shall go to have our portion in the Kingdom of the Blessed, where united in God we shall live and rejoice eternally together.

To the glory of that celestial Kingdom we are all invited—we, who ought everyone of us to be children in mind and heart—we are invited by Christ himself, who, as well by the outward word of His truth as by the interior inspiration of His grace unceasingly cries out to us—"Let the Little Children come to Me."

www.ingramcontent.com/pod-product-compliance
Lightning Source LLC
LaVergne TN
LVHW051709080426
835511LV00017B/2815